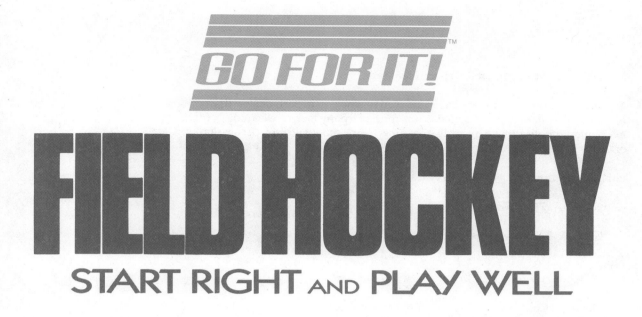

GO FOR IT!™

FIELD HOCKEY

START RIGHT AND PLAY WELL

by Bill Gutman
with Illustrations
by Ben Brown

MARSHALL CAVENDISH
CORPORATION

GREY CASTLE PRESS

Marshall Cavendish Edition, Freeport, New York.

Published by arrangement with Grey Castle Press, Lakeville, Ct.

The *GO FOR IT* Sports Series is a trademark of Grey Castle Press.

Printed in the USA

The Library of Congress Cataloging in Publication Data

Gutman, Bill.
     Field Hockey : start right and play well / by Bill Gutman ; with
illustrations by Ben Brown.
          p.   cm. — (Go for it!)
     Summary: Describes the history, current teams, leagues, and
championships of field hockey and provides instruction on how to
play the game.
     ISBN 0-942545-93-1 (lib. bdg.)
     1. Field Hockey—Juvenile literature. [1. Field Hockey.]
I. Brown, Ben, 1921–   Ill. II. Title. III. Series: Gutman, Bill.
Go for it!
GV1017.H7G87   1990
796.35′5—dc20   89-7587
                                                                         CIP
                                                                          AC

Photo Credits: Betty Shellenberger, page 7; U. S. Field Hockey Association,
page 6.

Special thanks to: Sue Smith, varsity field hockey coach, Dover Junior/Senior High
School, Dover Plains, N.Y.

Picture research: Omni Photo Communications, Inc.

ABOUT THE AUTHOR

Bill Gutman is the author of over 70 books for children and young adults. The majority of his titles have dealt with sports, in both fiction and non-fiction, including "how-to" books. His name is well-known to librarians who make it their business to be informed about books of special interest to boys and reluctant readers. He lives in Poughquag, New York.

ABOUT THE ILLUSTRATOR

Ben Brown's experience ranges from cartoonist to gallery painter. He is a graduate of the High School of Music & Art in New York City and the University of Iowa Art School. He has been a member of the National Academy of Design and the Art Students' League. He has illustrated government training manuals for the disadvantaged (using sports as themes), and his animation work for the American Bible Society won two blue ribbons from the American Film Festival. He lives in Great Barrington, Massachusetts.

In order to keep the instructions in this book as simple as possible, the author has chosen in most cases to use "he" to signify both boys and girls.

A BRIEF HISTORY

Games that looked something like field hockey were played in ancient countries thousands of years ago. That shouldn't be surprising. It was almost a natural thing for someone to take a stick and start hitting a round object with it.

There was a stick-and-ball game played in ancient Persia and in Greece that looked a lot like today's field hockey. But the modern form of the game began mainly in nineteenth century England. The first field hockey club was formed there sometime around mid-century. The club was called Blackheath and they called the game "hockie." The French also had a version known as "hoquet."

The English wrote the modern rules. It was also the English who began spreading the game worldwide. British sailors and teachers brought it to the various English colonies. The game became extremely popular in India, and later in Pakistan. These countries have dominated Olympic field hockey, especially the men's game.

The sport first came to the United States in 1901. It was brought over from England by a woman named Constance Applebee. She had come to study at Harvard College summer school. With a group of her fellow students, she organized the first game ever played in the U.S.

Constance Applebee went on to become known as "Miss

Anita Huntsman, right, a two-time United States Olympian, is a Hall of Fame player who has helped field hockey to grow in America. She has continued in the sport as a coach.

Hockey." She later went to Vassar College and introduced the game there. She also helped start field hockey programs at other colleges—Wellesley, Smith, Radcliffe, Mt. Holyoke and Bryn Mawr. Then, as now, the game in America was played mainly by girls and women.

By 1922, the sport had become so popular in the U.S. that the United States Field Hockey Association was organized. The USFHA also became part of the International Federation of Women's Field Hockey Association when that group was formed in 1927.

There were some fine players in those early years. In fact, one of America's greatest players was Anne Townsend. She became an All-American in 1924 and remained an outstanding player until 1939.

The sport continued to grow at the high school, college and club levels. But it wasn't until the 1970s that it really became a major sport for women. Perhaps it was helped by the passing of an amendment to the Civil Rights Act of 1964. The amendment was passed by Congress in 1972. It required colleges and universities to provide the same programs for women as they did for men. This act really started the sports boom for women at the college level.

By 1975, the National Collegiate Field Hockey Championship Tournament was held for the first time. There were 16 teams in the final round. Now the tournament is played each year the week before Thanksgiving, and has become a major part of the college sports scene.

The sport, however, has not been confined to women only. Men began playing in the United States in 1928. It was played at the club level, and the first team was organized by Henry Greer in Rye, New York. A year later, the Field Hockey Association of America (FHAA) was formed as the governing body of men's field hockey in America.

Anne B. Townsend (left) was one of the greatest field hockey players of all time. She was a captain and defensive star for the United States between 1923 and 1947. Her long and outstanding career also earned her a place in the Field Hockey Hall of Fame.

By 1932, there was a men's team good enough to win a bronze medal at the Olympic Games. But since that time, the U.S. men's teams have not done well internationally. The best was another bronze at the Pan-American Games in 1967.

The men's game did not spread as quickly as the women's because it was not played at the college level. For years it was played mainly around Philadelphia and New York. And only by club teams. It spread slowly, and in 1968 was played in California for the first time. Since then, there has been slow but steady growth. There are clubs in many states. Boys are now beginning to play more in junior high and high school, usually in co-educational physical education classes.

The women finally got their sport into the Olympics in 1980. But because of a boycott by the United States, the field hockey team didn't play. Then at the Los Angeles Olympics in 1984, the women's team took a bronze medal, finishing third behind Holland and West Germany. In 1988, the U.S. team qualified as one of the final eight teams, but failed to win a medal.

Today, the sport is still growing. Top high school players can earn full scholarships to schools that are highly competitive in field hockey. Worldwide, the sport is played by 60 percent men and 40 percent women. But in the United States it is still essentially a women's sport and a very popular one at that.

ORGANIZED FIELD HOCKEY

Although field hockey is not played as a professional sport in the United States, the USFHA has organized programs for women from six to 80. There are junior hockey programs in many parts of the country in which girls down to the age of six may play the game.

Most girls begin playing when they are in the eighth or ninth grade. It may be in gym classes or intramurals. The best girls will soon be playing junior varsity or varsity field hockey with their high school teams. Once again, the best players can go on, this time to college teams, where competition is intense.

But even though there are no professional leagues, a field hockey career does not have to end after college. There are many club teams for adults. Players can remain with these teams for many years. Before 1980, the USFHA allowed club teams to join local associations. There were then sectional tournaments open to these teams. The best players in these tournaments made the All-Sectional team.

From there, they went to a national tournament, which was held on Thanksgiving weekend in one of the nine different sections. The best 22 players were then chosen to be members of the United States First and Reserve teams.

Today there is an Olympic development program as well. The program is run at a series of camps that have four levels. The D level is open to mostly high school age players. The C level is open to college age players, and also to older players. The best of these players are invited to participate at the B level. And finally, the top 60 players are chosen for the A level. From this level, the Olympic team is chosen.

For a sport that is not played on the professional level, field hockey is well organized and growing. There is hope that it might even become popular with boys at the high school and college levels some day. Despite the fact that few men play the sport in the United States, the men's national team has been rated among the top 20 in the world.

The Sport Of Field Hockey

Field hockey is played on a large, grass field, usually 100 yards long and 60 yards wide. Each team consists of 10 players and a goalkeeper. The object of the game is to score a goal by moving a ball up the field with sticks and then shoot it into a goal. The goal is four yards wide and seven feet high.

The game is similar to soccer in that a ball is moved up and down the field and then shot into a goal at the end of the field. There are also attacking players, defenders and a goalkeeper. But in many other ways, field hockey has its own rules and certainly its own skills.

For example, a goal can be scored only if both attacking player and ball are inside the *striking circle*. The striking circle is a semi-circle that extends 16 yards around the goal. There can be no long shots or blasts that somehow get through the defense and past the goaltender. Teams must have the skills to work the ball into the striking area.

Other field markings include a solid center line, which divides

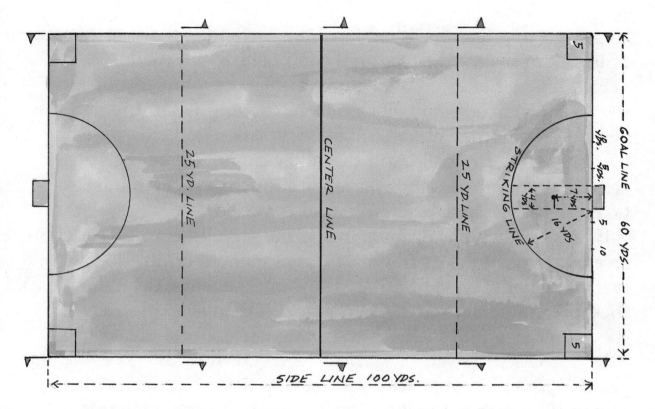

Field hockey is played on a large, grassy field, usually 100 yards long by 60 yards wide. The striking circle has a 16-yard radius and the goal is 12 feet wide and 7 feet high.

the field into two equal halves. There are two dotted, 25-yard lines, one on each side between the goal lines and center line. There are two other dotted lines five yards from the sidelines and running parallel with them. These five-yard areas are called *alleys*.

Games are divided into two halves of 30 to 35 minutes apiece, depending on the level of play. There is a five or ten minute halftime, during which the players change sides. There are two umpires, each taking one half of the field. And one or two timekeepers also work the game.

After a coin toss, the game begins with a maneuver called a "push-back." This takes place in the five-yard circle at the middle of the field. A player on the team with the ball must push it backward to a teammate to start play. Defenders have to remain outside the five-yard circle until the pushback in made.

Free hits are allowed after a player has been fouled outside the striking circle. The ball cannot be moving when the free hit is made. The other players must be at least five yards from the person hitting the ball. And the hitter cannot strike the ball a second time until another player has touched it. Free hits are taken from the spot where the foul occurred.

If an offensive player fouls inside the striking circle, the defensive team may take its free hit from anywhere on the 16-yard line. A penalty, or *short corner*, is awarded against defenders if they play the ball over their own goal line to stop play. Or if they commit a foul inside the striking circle.

In this case, the hit, or *pushout*, is taken from the goal line, 10 yards from the goal post. The attacking team can decide on which side of the post it will be taken. Five of the defenders may stand behind the goal line at least five yards from the ball. The other defensive players must stand beyond the half-way line until the hit is made. All attackers must be outside the striking circle. And a direct shot at goal cannot be taken until the ball is either stopped or controlled.

Another type of shot, called a *long hit*, is taken by an attacker from either the sideline or the goal line five yards from the corner flag on either side. It occurs when a defender plays the ball over the goal line, but does not do it on purpose. Defensive players must be at least five yards from the point of the hit.

When the ball goes out of bounds over the sideline, a *push-in* is called. That means the ball can only be pushed along the ground with all players at least five yards away. If the ball is hit or lofted, possession goes to the other team. At the high school level, however, it is not a foul to lift the ball off the ground during a push-in. But only a push or *flick stroke* may be used.

There is also an *offsides* call in field hockey. It occurs when an attacking player is nearer the opposing goal than two opponents and the ball.

Fouls leading to a free hit are called for the following violations:

1. A trip, push or charge into another player.
2. To hook, hit, hold or interfere with an opponent's stick.
3. Playing the ball with the rounded side of the stick.
4. Stopping the ball in the air with any part of the body other than the hand.
5. Using the foot or leg to support the stick; or to use the hand or any other part of the body to pick up, hold, throw, carry or move the ball.
6. Raising any part of the stick above the shoulders when playing the ball.
7. Striking or touching an opponent with the stick or body.
8. Undercutting or lifting the ball in a dangerous way.

A penalty stroke is awarded when a defensive player intentionally violates the rules within the striking circle. A penalty stroke is also given if the defense commits a foul to stop what would have been an almost certain goal. The player taking the penalty stroke gets a free shot seven yards from the center of the goal. It's only the shooter and goalkeeper, no one else.

The stroke must be either a *push*, *flick* or *scoop*. A *hit* (which is a much more powerful stroke) is not allowed. And the player can only take one step before shooting. In addition, the stick cannot be raised above the shoulders or the stroke will be disallowed and the defensive team will get a free hit.

These are just some of the rules, violations, and special plays that a new player will have to learn. They may seem complicated now. But the more you work with your new teammates, the more you will understand about how field hockey is played.

The Positions

As in soccer, there are three different types of positions in field hockey. The *goalkeeper*, of course, is separate. The other groups are *attackers*, *midfielders* (sometimes called *links*) and *defenders*. Each has different jobs to do during the game. Here, briefly, are descriptions of each of the positions.

Every team, of course, should have a good goalkeeper. The goalie should be a very quick, alert player. She should always be in tip-top physical condition and must concentrate on the game at all times. She must be able to kick the ball out with either foot and use the stick to move the ball to teammates. The goalie must also be able to play under pressure and make the big save with the game on the line.

The defenders play closest to the goalkeeper. In several popular formations there are just two *back defenders*, as they are called. They get help from the three *midfielders*, or *halfbacks*. Back defenders have to be good tacklers. That is, they must be able to take the ball away from attackers. And they have to pass well to help their team go from defense to attack as quickly as possible.

Defenders should learn to support the attack as soon as it starts. They must also be able to play both zone and man-to-man defense. In zone, they will cover a specific area of the field. With man-to-man, they must take a specific player and follow her no matter where she goes.

Back defenders should work together. They must talk, direct traffic in front of them, and cover for each other whenever necessary. They must also have enough speed to move up field with an attack. But, if necessary, they have to get back quickly to stop a possible breakaway. The one thing a back defender must try to avoid is passing the ball across the front of her own goal. Even if a teammate is on the other side, an attacker could intercept the pass and score.

Halfbacks must be able to play both offense and defense. There are usually three halfbacks, a *center halfback* and two *wing halfs*. Their primary job is to control play in the middle of the field. But they must also be able to get back on defense to stop an attack. After that, they should be able to rush up field and become a smooth-working part of their own attack.

All halfbacks must always be in excellent physical condition. There is a great deal of running involved in switching from offense to defense during the game. Of the three halfbacks, the center halfback is usually the best defensive player on the team.

Her job is to cover the opposing center forward, as well as the center of the field. She must be able to move the ball to both the left and right, and also to support any other defensive player who needs help.

The two wing halfbacks must be fast enough to *mark*, or guard, the opposing wings. Both should be good dribblers and ball handlers. They must also pass well and be able to mark and *tackle*. Wing halfbacks must understand the game completely. They must know when to drop back to cover for a back defender who has moved up. And like the center halfback, the wings must be in excellent physical condition at all times.

With two back defenders and three halfbacks, that leaves five players for the forward slots. The two forwards who play up and down the sideline are called *wing forwards*. The wings should have great speed and the ability to move the ball with that speed. That means good ball handling skills. They must also be able to make sharp, accurate passes to the center of the field. And this takes practice.

The two wing forwards often play in the five-yard alley along the sideline to make sure the attack is always spread out. If they move inside, the middle of the field will get too crowded and that makes it easier to defend. The wings must help on defense and work together with the *inside forward* nearest them and also with the wing halfback.

One of the toughest spots on the field to play is at inside forward. A big part of the job is to pave the way for the center forward and the wings. In the "five-forward front," the inside forwards play slightly behind the other three, giving the formation the look of a "W." Usually, the *inside right* is more of a playmaker, while the *inside left* is more of a scorer.

In this system, the inside right will combine with the wing and center to work the ball down the right side of the field. The inside left will be more on the receiving end of passes from the right. She will usually try to take these passes at the top of the striking circle. Therefore, she must be quick, have good stick-

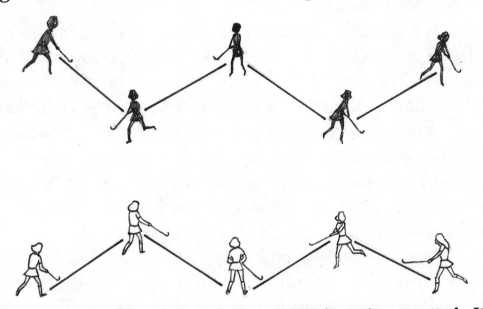

A very basic formation is called the 5-3-2, or the "W" formation, on attack. It is called the "M" formation on defense. The "W" is formed by the two wings and center forward up front, plus the two insides, who back up the slots between them. The center halfback can also come up to help on offense. When the center half drops back, the "M" on defense is formed. She joins the wing halfbacks and two fullbacks, who move to mark the opposing inside forwards.

16

work, and a hard, accurate shot. The two inside forwards often take the ball and work it upfield to key the attack.

The center forward is a very important part of the attack. She must be a very fast player, especially for quick, 10-yard bursts. She often moves diagonally back and forth across the center of the field. This is either to make room for other players or free herself for a pass and shot.

All center forwards must be good shooters. In addition to a hard shot, they must be able to shoot quickly in heavy traffic—that is, from different angles, under pressure and off balance.

Center forwards should have a strong flick and hit. There are also times when the center forward will switch positions with a wing who is cutting into the middle. The center forward must have the skills to do this, then get back into position quickly.

There are certain skills that all field hockey players must have. Some positions demand more of one skill than another, but a player who can do everything well will help her team more.

Uniform And Equipment

The basic field hockey uniform consists of either a kilt or shorts, with a cotton blouse. Many teams prefer to wear kilts. The loose-fitting garments give the players plenty of freedom of movement. If a team is wearing shorts instead of the kilts, the shorts should also be loose fitting and comfortable.

When the weather is cold, several things can be added to the basic uniform. Girls can wear gloves, tights or knee socks, and sweaters to keep warm. Sometimes, in fact, the sport is played on a frozen field. In that case, players may want to wear sneakers instead of their regular shoes with cleats.

Many players today wear a lightweight leather soccer shoe. Most have rubber or plastic cleats, which give better traction under most field conditions. Shoes can be waterproofed and should always be kept clean. Dirt should be removed from the cleats after every practice and game. The leather can be kept clean with any kind of cleaner or leather soap. Shoes must be comfortable and well-fitting. A young player should always try to buy the best shoes she can afford.

It is also advisable for players to wear shin guards. However, everyone *must* use a mouthpiece. The shin guards are similar to those used in soccer. They are flat pieces of plastic that fit inside the high socks. They can prevent bruising if a player is accidentally hit in the shin with a stick. Mouthpieces are molded pieces of clear plastic that fit over the teeth, protecting both teeth and mouth from injury.

The goalkeepers also wear special pieces of equipment. They

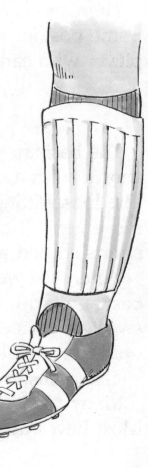

Shin guards are flat pieces of plastic that are worn between two pairs of socks. Players are advised to wear them because the lightweight shinguard can keep a player from getting a bad bruise if she is acidentally hit with a stick.

usually wear pads that cover the thighs, legs and insteps. The pads are buckled to the leg, but are hinged at the knee so they don't stop the goalie from moving quickly. Padded overshoes called "kickers" also help to protect the feet and insteps of the goalkeepers.

Goalies generally wear a cleated shoe, but one with a boxed toe for kicking the ball. The shoes should be large enough for an extra pair of wool socks in the cold weather. If the goalie wears gloves, they should not hinder the use of the stick. But goalies must be warm during cold weather, even it it means wearing a warm-up suit. After all, the goalie does not do the running that the other players do.

A helmet, with or without a facemask, is optional. Many coaches feel that a facemask will soon be a requirement for all goalies.

That brings us to the final two items that are necessary for a field hockey game—the ball and the stick. In some ways, the ball is much like a baseball. It has a cork center that is wound with twine. The cover is made of leather. There is also a less expensive ball, covered with plastic. It is good for practice and for playing on wet fields, but the leather ball is the official one.

The ball weighs between 5 1/2 and 5 3/4 ounces and is between 2 7/8 and 3 3/8 inches in diameter. The leather balls usually last just a season, since they tend to crack if kept in a hot place.

Then there is the stick. This is perhaps the most important piece of equipment a player will have. A field hockey stick has to feel right to each player. That comes from a combination of weight and balance. For a stick to have good balance, the weight must be well-distributed between the handle and the head. Weight for college-age players is usually between 18 and 21 ounces. Younger players should choose a stick between 17 and 19 ounces.

The handle and back side of the field hockey stick is rounded. The bottom part of the blade side is flat. Most sticks are 30 to 36 inches long and are made of wood. The handles of the better sticks are made from cane and contain several rubber inserts. The ball has a cork center that is wound with twine. The outer covering is leather and the entire ball is between 2 7/8 and 3/38 inches in diameter.

Most sticks range from 30 to 36 inches in length. When a player is picking out a stick, she should take her normal grip and swing. The head of the stick should just brush the grass. If the stick is too long, the player will hit behind the ball. If it's too short, she will top the ball and have to bend over far too much.

With quality sticks, the grain of the wood follows the curve of the head (or blade). The handle of the better sticks is made of cane and has a large number of little holes at the top of the handle. There are also three rubber inserts in the handle. The less expensive sticks have only one or two inserts. This limits the flexibility of the stick. It doesn't absorb as much vibration from hard drives, something you can really feel on cold days.

But whether you can afford the best stick or not, make sure the one you get feels comfortable and is easy to handle. That's the most important thing at first.

It is wise to put some linseed oil on the stick at the start of a season. Do it again several times during the schedule. That will stop moisture from getting in the grain. Wet or damp sticks should be wiped off right after practice or the game. Dampness can ruin a good stick very quickly. Warm weather can also cause the rubber grips to dry out.

It's important to have good equipment and know how to care

for it. A good coach will get a new player started in the right direction. But now comes the most important part of all. That is learning the skills that will make you a real field hockey player.

Getting Ready To Play

As with all sports, a player should not start a new season without getting ready. To go out for a team when you have not done anything to prepare yourself is a very bad idea. First of all, someone not in good physical condition can get hurt much more easily. Secondly, a young player in poor physical condition just will not be able to keep up with her teammates. She might not even be able to run through the drills.

Before the season even starts, anyone planning to play field hockey should be running. In fact, it's probably a good idea to run two or three miles at least three times a week. It doesn't have to be hard running. But it should be at a pace that leaves you pretty tired when you finish. This is necessary if you want to build up your stamina.

Along with distance running, a player getting ready for field hockey might want to run some wind sprints. This means running very hard for 10 or 15 yards, stopping, then exploding for another 10 or 15. By doing this a number of times, a player does two things. She helps build endurance and stamina. And she gets used to the stop-and-start running of the sport itself.

It is also a good idea for young players to do some general fitness exercises. They will tone and stretch muscles and get the player ready for action. Jumping rope, situps, pushups or modified pushups will all help with coordination and conditioning. Stretching exercises should also become part of your daily workout.

Your coach will show you stretching exercises to loosen up leg and back muscles, which will reduce the chances for being injured. Remember, all stretching exercises should be done slowly. They should be held from five to 10 seconds at the point of maximum stretch. Yet there should be no pain or discomfort. If there is, then stop.

Your running and exercise program should be combined with good everyday habits. Young athletes should always be sure to eat right and get plenty of rest. That means not too much junk food, lots of fresh fruits, juices, and vegetables—a balanced diet. Budget your time with schoolwork and chores. And NEVER use tobacco, alcohol or drugs!

If you do all these things and are willing to give field hockey your best effort, then you are ready to play.

LEARNING HOW TO PLAY FIELD HOCKEY

Learning How To Dribble

The field hockey stick is flat on one side, rounded on the other. The rules say that only the flat side of the stick may be used to strike the ball. In addition, all sticks are made to be used on the right side of the player. That makes left-handed sticks illegal. So all players, even lefthanders, must grip the stick the same way and strike the ball on the right side.

Lefthanders, however, don't usually have a problem with this. In fact, with the field hockey grip, the left hand controls a good many of the strokes.

For the basic grip, a player will hold the stick in her right hand with the flat side facing left. The left hand is placed above the right at the top of the handle. The grip is like a handshake. Now, holding the stick, the player will turn it so that the flat side faces forward and the stick is perpendicular to the ground.

The right hand is placed a few inches below the left. The fingers of both hands are then wrapped around the stick. The lower the right hand is held on the stick, the more control the player has. But the higher the hand, the easier it is to run and move and see the field. Veteran players usually place the right hand fairly close to the left, so the head can be held higher and the player can see the field better.

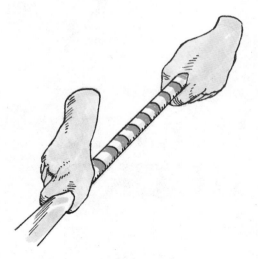

A field hockey player should grip the lower part of the stick in her right hand. The flat side of the stick should face left. Then she puts her left hand on the top of the stick and shakes hands with it. From this position, the right hand can move up and down on the stick and the left hand can control it for different types of hits and strokes.

A young player has to be careful not to slide the left hand around the stick so that the fingernails face forward. If this happens, the player may be unable to control the stick and execute many of the strokes. A number of these strokes depend on the correct grip if they are to be done right.

When a player is not directly involved in the action, she can carry her stick in her right hand. The hand should be halfway down the stick with the head up. That will allow her to use her arms and run naturally. As she gets closer to the play, she can bring her left hand back to the top of the stick and she's just about ready to hit.

There are also some basic rules of movement. Once again, this is similar to soccer. When a player is handling the ball or moving to receive a pass, she should take short, brisk strides. That makes changing direction and cutting easier. And it makes it easier to control the ball on the dribble. Longer strides can be taken in the open field when a player is a distance from the ball. Naturally, longer strides cover more ground. But they are not a good idea in heavy traffic, especially when the player is dribbling the ball.

Good field hockey players can dribble the ball in every direction. The object, of course, is to move it downfield. But being

Each player must learn to carry the stick in a balanced, comfortable way. She has to be able to run freely with the stick, yet be ready to handle the ball if it should come her way.

able to control the ball on the stick allows a player to avoid defenders trying to steal the ball.

Begin with the basic grip. Then flex the left arm so that the forearm becomes almost an extension of the stick. When the left wrist is relaxed, the stick should then extend to the ground just in front of the right foot. The relaxed wrist will also give the player more control because she can quickly rotate her wrists. The left hand and arm do most of the controlling. The right hand does not exert any force. It basically guides the stick.

There are several types of dribbling. In the open field, with no defenders around, a player may want to use what is sometimes called the "loose dribble." This is simply tapping the ball a short distance in front of your body, then running after it and tapping it again. This dribble will allow a player to move faster. But if there are defenders around, they can easily take it away. Also, if a player wants to make a quick pass, the ball may be too far in

This is the proper way to hold the stick for the basic "loose" dribble. The player will tap the ball a short distance in front of her, then run after it and tap it again. This dribble is used when the player is in the open field and not closely guarded.

front to make the pass. The opportunity may be lost. So use the loose dribble only when you're sure it's the best thing to do.

To dribble close to defenders, you must move the ball back and forth across the front of your body. This is called the "Indian dribble" and is much like the way an ice hockey player dribbles the puck. But remember, in field hockey, only the flat side of the stick may be used.

With your right hand down on the stick, lean forward with your head over the ball. Then begin by tapping the ball to the left, using just the face of the stick. You move it to the side, but also a short distance in front of you. As you step after it, turn the stick with your left hand, rotating it in your loose right hand.

Then reach for the ball with the "reverse stick" and move it back to the right and slightly ahead of you. Taking short steps, you should be able to control the ball with this basic movement. By not hitting the ball too far in front of you, you'll also be ready to change direction quickly. And the ball will be right there if you decide to pass.

26

Control of the stick is very important. You must be good at turning the stick with the left hand to get the reverse stick on the ball. This movement has to become almost second nature to all field hockey players.

There will also be times when an opponent will challenge you for the ball. If there isn't an open teammate waiting for a pass, you may have to try to dribble around your opponent. As with other sports where a dribble is involved, a player must be able to fake going one way, then quickly move in the other direction. In field hockey, this is called *dodging*.

With dodging, timing is very important. If a player starts a dodge move too soon, the defender can be ready. If it is started too late, the defender may try a tackle. Another thing to remember is to try to take the defender by surprise. If you slow down, it should be an attempt to draw the defender toward you. Then a quick acceleration and you may get past her.

The most common dodges are the *push to the right* and the *pull to the left*. These are usually the first a new player learns. The push to the right is usually done on the right side of the field. That's because the defender sometimes plays to the left, expecting a pass. The dodge begins by angling the dribble to the left to get the opponent moving that way. Then, as the opponent moves for the ball, the attacker pushes the ball to the right and past her. She then runs to the left of her opponent and recovers the ball behind her.

The pull-to-the-left dodge is usually used on the left side of the field. The left dodge is started like the right, by moving the ball to get the defender to lean the wrong way. In this case, it's moved right, then quickly pulled back to the left. But this time it isn't tapped past the defender. Rather it is carried by the dribble. It must be done quickly, with fast stickwork needed to turn the stick sideways then forward. Good acceleration is also necessary.

The push to the right, or right dodge, is most often done on the right side of the field. That's because the defender is often looking for the pass to the left. The dribbler will angle the ball to the left, or even fake a pass. Then, as her opponent moves for the ball, she suddenly pushes it to the right, past her opponent.

As her opponent moves for the ball, the attacker makes a quick move to the left, races past her opponent, and recovers the ball.

With the *lift dodge*, the attacker actually lofts the ball about six inches off the ground and over the defender's stick. The attacker then steps to the side of the defender and picks the ball up again. This should be done quickly, because the stick must be angled down to lift the ball and the defender can see it coming.

A reverse stick dodge can also be used. For example, a player may fake a pull to the left dodge. She begins to push the ball left, then reverses her stick and brings it back to the right. If the defender leans the wrong way, the attacker can go past her.

These types of moves take a great deal of practice. A player must be able to "feel" the ball on the end of her stick and not watch it constantly. That way, she can see the field ahead of her and be ready to deal with a defender or make a pass.

Many coaches feel that too much dribbling will slow an attack. Generally, a good team will pass more than it dribbles. But there are still times when a player will have to handle the ball. When that happens, she has to know how to do it. That means controlling the ball straight ahead, side to side, and in traffic.

The lift dodge can be used when a tackler is coming right at you. There is no faking involved, so good timing is important. When you're ready to make your move, start by drawing the top of the stick backward. You're now in position to lift the ball over the stick of the defender.

The lift is made with a quick flick. The ball should only go about six inches off the ground, just enough to clear your opponent's stick.

Now quickness really counts. Once the ball is in the air and over your opponent's stick, you have to dart around her and pick up the ball again before she can react and change direction. Quickness and good stick handling are both important parts of the lift dodge.

A dodge that takes a great deal of practice is the reverse stick dodge. The attacker begins by pushing the ball left, as if she is trying to push it past the defender.

When the defender moves to intercept the ball, the attacker quickly reverses her stick and brings the ball back to the right.

With her opponent off balance, the attacker then pushes the ball to the right, past her opponent, and follows quickly after it.

Learning How To Stop And Receive The Ball

Before a field hockey player can dribble, pass or even shoot, she must learn to receive and stop the ball. There are some very special skills needed to do this, using both the stick and hand. It is important to know the best technique for each instance.

The object in stopping and receiving is to control the ball as quickly as possible. The faster a player controls it, the faster she can continue or go on the attack. According to the rules, a ball may be stopped with the hand only while it is in the air. If the ball is stopped in the air by the hand, it must drop directly to the ground after contact. So the hand can only be used as a stop. It cannot push, shove, deflect or move the ball in another direction.

The ball in the air is often better stopped by hand. In fact, it is illegal to stop a ball higher than your shoulder with the stick. If a ball is coming toward you, cup your hand and hold it out in front of you. As the ball makes contact, draw your hand back, "giving" with the ball. Then uncup the hand at almost the same time. This will do two things. It will cause the ball to drop straight down and also keep your hand from being hurt. Then wait until the ball hits the ground before playing it.

If the ball is below the waist, you can still play it with your

Left. A ball in the air can be stopped with the hand, too. The hand should be cupped and held out in front. As the ball makes contact, draw your hand back to cushion the impact. However, the ball must drop straight to the ground after contact. You cannot direct it to one side or the other. Remember, a ball coming in higher than the shoulder cannot be stopped with the stick. *Right.* Uncup your hand at the same time the ball hits. Then, direct the ball straight down and follow through with your hand. The ball cannot be played with the stick until it hits the ground.

hand. Use the same technique, but hold the cupped hand downward instead of upward.

One other thing to be remembered about a hand stop. Never take your eyes off the ball until it is in your hand. Look at it all the way.

There may also be times when you will want to stop the ball in the air with the stick. Rule number one: make sure the stick stays below shoulder height. If the ball is coming straight at you, keep the stick straight up and down. This gives you the greatest amount of stick area with which to stop the ball. It also cuts down the chances of a deflection.

Once again, watch the ball carefully. Hold the left hand at the top of the stick and the right hand well down on the shaft. The right hand should grip the stick loosely. This, too, cuts down the chance of a deflection. Then move the left hand forward just

If a ball is coming right at you in the air, be sure to keep your stick straight up and down. This cuts down on the chance of a deflection. Hold your left hand at the top of the stick and your right hand far down the shaft. Once again, your right hand should have just a loose grip on the stick. By moving your left hand forward, you create an angle to allow the ball to drop straight down. Contact the ball on the flat part of the stick and play it as soon as it hits the ground.

A ball coming in the air from the side, but not above the shoulder, can be stopped with the stick. This takes timing and a great deal of practice. Start by holding the stick parallel to the ground. If possible, hold your right hand near the middle of the stick. The farther you must reach, the farther up the stick you have to keep your right hand. As the ball hits the flat part of the stick, draw the stick backward. This will allow the ball to drop straight down and not rebound. Because the ball in the illustration is coming from the player's right, she must use the reverse stick technique to make the stop.

enough to allow ball to drop straight down. Once the ball is on the ground, control it with the head of the stick.

A ball coming from the side across your body is a little tougher to stop with the stick. In a way, it's almost like bunting a softball. This time the stick is held parallel to the ground. Again the right hand is well down the stick. Catch the ball on the flat part of the stick below the right hand. As the ball makes contact, draw the stick back to cushion the impact and avoid a rebound. As the ball drops, move quickly to control it.

When the ball is coming from right to left, the reverse stick technique must be used. That is, the head is pointed down so contact will again be made on the flat side.

Receiving and stopping the ball on the ground takes a slightly different technique. If the ball is coming toward you, make sure your body is directly in the path of the ball. The stick should be kept upright, with the head on the ground. This will give you the largest possible flat area with which to stop the ball.

Once again, keep the right hand loose on the stick. The left hand then moves the top of the stick forward. This leaves the stick at an angle to stop the ball as soon as contact is made. You don't want a rebound. You want immediate control. And be sure to "watch" the ball right onto the stick.

The technique is slightly different when receiving a ball from either side. The important thing is to avoid a rebound. If there

To receive a ball coming directly at you on the ground, start by placing your body in front of the incoming ball. Keep your right hand loose on the stick and move the top of the stick forward with your left hand. This will create an angle to stop the ball as soon as it hits the stick, giving you immediate control. Remember, if the ball bounces off the stick, it could rebound to an opponent. You can also move the head of the stick backward just as the ball arrives. This will cushion the contact and keep the ball in front of you.

is a slight rebound, you want it to be straight in front of the stick. You don't want it to be off to one side or the other.

This can be done by always making sure your stick is held out on the line of the ball. That means if the ball were to run up the length of the stick, it would still go on a straight line, only

Stopping a ball that is coming from the side takes a separate technique. As the ball comes at you, make sure that your stick is held on the line of the ball. In other words, the head of the stick should be out over the ball.

As the ball arrives, draw the head of the stick back to cushion the contact. If you bring the stick straight back, you should stop the ball right in front of you with no rebound. If the ball comes from the right, use the same technique, but with the reverse stick. That way, the flat side will still make the stop.

upwards. The right hand should again be a little below the left, with the head of the stick out over the ball.

As the ball arrives, move the head of the stick backward to cushion the contact. If the head is out over the ball with the stick in line, just bring the head straight back as the contact is made. That way the ball should stop right in front of you. If the ball comes from the right, the same technique is used. Only the head of the stick is turned down and the flat side still makes the stop.

Learning How To Shoot And Pass

A number of basic strokes in field hockey are used for both shooting and passing. There are times during a game when a certain stroke is the best one to use. In fact, the only one. That's why every young player must learn and practice these strokes.

The most popular stroke in field hockey is the hit, or drive. Every player should be able to make a quick, accurate hit. Begin by placing both hands together near the top of the stick. As you step into the ball with your left foot, bring the stick back. But be sure not to raise it above your shoulder. At the top of the backswing, your wrists can be cocked upward to add power to the swing.

Perhaps the most popular stroke is the *hit*, or *drive*. It can be used for both long and short passes and also for shooting at the goal. The smart player will soon learn when to use the hit.

To make a proper hit, the hands should be placed together near the top of the stick. Step into the hit with the left foot, placing it alongside and six inches from the ball. Remember, the stick cannot be raised above the shoulder on the backswing. Bring the stick back as you step into the ball. If your hands are

Left. As with swings in other sports, your hips and shoulders should turn into the hit first. The left arm then starts the stick moving downward and the right arm helps guide it, then supplies much of the power. Contact should be made with the arms straight and wrists firm. **Right.** As the swing is made, your weight is transferred from the rear foot to the front foot. After contact, you must complete the swing by following through. The stick should follow the path of the ball as the weight shift is completed. Your follow through should be smooth, but be sure not to take the stick above shoulder level.

not together, you can slide them together during the backswing. At the top of the backswing, the wrists should be cocked upward, so they can help to propel the stick through the swing.

The shoulders and hips should turn into the hit first. They should move in the direction you want to send the ball. The left arm starts the stick in the right direction. The right arm continues to guide it and then supplies a good deal of the force. The stroke is made with the arms straight and wrists firm. As with other stick swings (baseball, hockey, golf), the weight is transferred from rear to front foot as the swing is made.

To complete the hit, you must follow through. The stick should follow the path of the ball as you complete the weight transfer to your front foot. Once again, the follow through cannot take the stick above shoulder level.

As with all field hockey strokes, a player must also know how to make a reverse hit. That means stroking the ball from left to right with the head of the stick pointing toward the ground. This is a more difficult hit to make because it is harder to control. Some coaches tell their players to try to avoid the reverse hit, except when it is really necessary.

Once again, hands should be close together near the top. This time the player steps forward with the right foot. The distance is the same as with the regular hit, about six inches from the ball. Keep the right arm and stick in a straight line with your head over the ball. The weight transfer and the follow through are the same as before.

The reverse shot is not as accurate because there is less surface of the stick to make contact. It takes a great deal of practice to make the reverse shot well. Players must also practice running to the ball and making the drive in a smooth motion. And there will be times when the hit has to be made as the ball is moving. There are a number of ways this can be done.

Left. The reverse hit is more difficult because the ball is harder to control. The hit is made from left to right, with the head of the stick pointed toward the ground. The technique is basically the same one described earlier. Your hands should be held together high on the stick as you step into the hit with your front foot. The stick is kept in a straight line with the ball. *Right.* With the reverse hit, there is not as much stick surface to contact the ball. But the hit should still be made with your arms straight and wrists firm. This is necessary for maximum control. Always keep your eye on the ball, head down, until you are well into your follow through.

That's why it can't be learned overnight. Good players must also be able to control the speed of the hit. There are times when you will want to hit the ball very hard. But other times, you'll have to hold back. Your form must be the same, but you've got to learn to control the speed and power in your swing. It takes a good touch to do this.

There will be times when a teammate is so close to you that

the hit is not the best way to pass. In fact, the *push*, or *push pass*, is probably the most accurate way to pass the ball over a short distance. The push can also be used to make an accurate shot if you are close to the goal. It's a move that can be made quickly before the defense can tell what you are going to do.

Unlike the hit, the push is made with the hands apart on the stick. The left hand is near the top, but the right is well down on the stick. Because the push is made quickly, there is no backswing. The stick starts on the ball and in front of the body. When making the push, the player should lean forward from the waist and have the left foot well forward.

The left hand at the top of the stick acts almost like a lever. The right hand gives the push its power as it pushes the stick through the ball. The head should again be kept down and the follow through should be with knees bent and in the direction of the ball.

Another basic stroke in field hockey is the push. It is made with the hands held apart on the stick. There is also no backswing because the stroke must be made quickly. When making the push, the player should lean forward at the waist and have her left foot well forward. Her left hand acts almost like a lever. Her right hand gives the stroke its power as it pushes the stick through the ball.

While the push is usually made off the left foot, players must at times learn to make the push pass off either foot. They must also learn the reverse stick push with the head of the stick down. Unlike the reverse hit, the reverse push is a good pass to use. Because the stick begins on the ball, the reverse push can be very accurate.

It is done with the same technique, only in the opposite direction, left to right. When the reverse push is made, the stick should be kept as low to the ground as possible for the most accuracy.

As with all reverse stick plays, the stick should be rotated over the top with the left hand. The right hand does not turn. This is a common mistake new players make. If the right hand turns, it cannot direct the shot as well.

The stroke is made mostly off the left foot. Once again, the player's head should be kept down until after the push has been completed, and the follow through should leave the stick below shoulder level.

43

A third way to shoot or pass the ball is with the *flick*. This is used to raise the ball off the ground. It can be used to shoot, to pass the ball over the stick of a defender, or to lift the ball right over the opposing defense. Because the ball is lifted in the air, the flick is a very hard shot or pass for the defense to intercept.

One trick is to keep the ball on the stick as long as possible. The flick cannot be rushed, especially when a player is just learning the stroke. It must be made slowly, but firmly. With the flick, the hands are kept well apart on the stick, the left hand near the top. The feet should be wide apart, left foot forward. This will give the player balance.

With the flick, the body must be kept very low by bending at the knees. The stick makes contact with the ball in front of the left foot. The left hand and forearm move up on the ball first. As they do, the player straightens her right leg to add power and begins to transfer her weight from the right leg to the left.

The head of the stick is placed very low on the ball. This is so the ball can actually be cupped on the stick for an instant. The stroke is made with a kind of lever action. The right arm is held straight. Then the left hand snaps back and the right hand forward. This motion moves the stick upward and gives the ball its rise.

All the weight should be on the left leg at the follow through. Be sure not to bring the stick up too high. Keep your head down until the stroke has been made and concentrate on a strong, short movement of the hands and arms. Done right, the flick can travel 25 yards or more in the air.

The final basic stroke is the *scoop*. It is used to lift the ball over a group of players or a tight defensive line. The object is to have the ball land in an open area. The stroke has been called a lifting and throwing stroke. It can be used as an offensive move and once in a while as a shot to catch the goalkeeper by sur-

Still another popular stroke is the flick. The purpose of the flick is to get the ball off the ground and lift it over the defense. To do this, the player must keep her stick on the ball as long as possible. Her hands are well spread on the stick, feet wide apart and body low, legs bent at the knees. The stick will contact the ball in front of the player's left foot.

The head of the stick should be placed very low on the ball, actually cupping it for an instant. The stroke itself is a lever action. With her right arm held straight, the player snaps her left hand back and her right hand forward. Done right, this will make the stick move upward and cause the ball to rise. All the player's weight should be on her left leg during the follow through. Her head, of course, should be kept down until the stroke has been made.

45

prise. Or it can be used as a defensive move to get the ball out of a dangerous situation.

A player can make the scoop standing still, if the ball is rolling toward her. Or she can run to the ball, if it is not moving. When both the players and ball are moving, the scoop becomes a lot more difficult.

The scoop is made with the ball directly in front of the player. The feet should be apart, knees bent slightly, right foot about 12 inches in front of the left. Hands are held apart on the stick and the head is placed right behind the ball. The trick is to incline the stick backward to about a 50 degree angle to the ball (see illustration). That's what will give the ball its lift.

The stoke is made by moving your weight forward and keeping the stick in contact with the ball as long as possible. You are actually throwing the ball forward and up, not hitting it. It is

The final basic stroke is the scoop, used to lift the ball over a group of players. It is made with the ball directly in front of the player. The shot is made with feet apart, knees bent slightly and the right foot in front of the left. The player's hands are once again held apart. When the head of the stick is placed behind the ball, it should be at about a 50 degree angle. The angle is what gives the ball its lift. The stroke is made by keeping the stick in contact with the ball as long as possible, using a motion that throws the ball forward and up. The player's arms should be straight and wrists firm. Again, her head must be kept down until the follow through.

the right arm that throws the ball in the air. The arm movement should be straight, with the wrist firm. Remember to keep your head down and follow through. But don't raise the stick above your shoulder.

One reason the scoop sometimes gives young players trouble is the placement of the stick on the ball at the proper angle. If the angle is too low and the stick is too close to the ground, it may slip under the ball. If the angle is too high, the player won't get the kind of lift she is looking for. So it takes regular practice to learn the scoop and do it well.

The basic field hockey strokes are not difficult. But they must be practiced until they become second nature. If the strokes are almost automatic, the player can then put all her thoughts into the game. Perhaps the hardest part of learning the passing and shooting strokes is knowing the proper time to use each one.

Learning How To Tackle

Tackling in field hockey, as in soccer, means taking the ball away from an opponent. As a rule, a tackle should be made the moment the opponent gets the ball. Once the ball is being controlled, then the defender has to be more careful. She should jockey a bit, trying to force the opponent to make a move. Then, as soon as the opponent's stick is off the ball, she can go for the tackle.

No player can be successful with a tackle all the time. In fact, it's said that if two players have the same ability, the tackler will get the ball about half the time. But even if a good tackler doesn't come away with the ball, she can help her team. For in trying for the tackle, she may force a bad pass or a lost dribble.

But it still takes good judgement and timing to make a tackle. A missed tackle that takes you out of the play could help your opponents to score a goal. So, as a defender, you must be aware of the position of all the players on the field and decide if the time is right to go for the tackle.

There are a number of basic tackles that every player must know. The first is called the *straight tackle*. It is made with the tackler face to face with her opponent. The technique can be used by a defensive player to stop an attacker who is dribbling the ball. And it can be used by a forward to stop a defender who has just intercepted a pass.

The tackler should approach the dribbler carefully. If she rushes forward, a good dribbler can fake and dodge around her. Instead, she must follow the line of the ball moving side to side with the dribbler. Then she can begin to threaten the dribbler with her stick.

But sooner or later, the tackler must pick her spot. As the dribbler takes her stick away from the ball, the tackler should

The most basic type of defensive tackle is the straight tackle. It is made with the defender (right) facing the attacker. The straight tackle is generally used when the attacker is dribbling the ball. The tackler should approach the dribbler carefully, so she does not fall victim to a dodge. She should follow the ball closely, moving side to side with the dribbler.

put her weight on her left or front foot and lunge forward to get the ball. She must also be able to stop herself quickly. If she does get the ball, she has to be able to control it and make a move to secure it. That might mean moving quickly to the left or right with her own dribble. Or she may even want to pivot around.

The tackler can also get the ball and go right past her opponent, shoulder to shoulder. That's one reason to lead with the left foot. It helps bring the shoulder and hip forward, and this can help avoid a collision.

A move similar to the straight tackle is the *jab*. The technique is just about the same. But the object of the jab is to first poke the ball away from your opponent with your stick. Then you can try to control it. The jab is often used near or in the striking circle to poke the ball away from an attacker getting ready to shoot. It can also be used to poke a loose ball away from an opponent, giving your team a better chance to control it.

The jab is usually a one-handed stroke. It can be made with either hand, from both the front and side. The hand should be

The tackler must make her move when the dribbler takes her stick away from the ball. If she knocks it away, she has to be ready to battle for it. When she gets the ball on her stick, she must move quickly to control it and put her team on offense.

near the top of the stick. That will allow you to reach out farther. The weight should be on the leg closest to the direction in which you are reaching. The wrist should be kept firm and the stick close to the ground.

A skilled player will jab at the ball and then try to control it. You shouldn't poke at it without a plan. Either try to push it toward a teammate or into an open area where you can get it. Like the straight tackle, the jab takes timing, quickness and lots of practice.

Another method of tackling is the *open-side tackle*, also called the *left-hand lunge*. It is used at one time or another by every player on the field. Attackers often use this tackle to try to regain the ball after they have lost it to the defense. The lunge

The open-side tackle, or left-hand lunge, is one way to get the ball away from an attacker. The lunge is made by a defender running alongside the attacker. The first move is usually made with just one hand on the stick because the defender can reach farther that way. Running with her opponent, she will bring the stick down firmly as soon as she feels she can reach the ball.

can be made with one or two hands on the stick. However, the one-hand lunge is used more often because it gives players an extra few inches of reach. That can be important.

When you think you can make an open-side tackle, you must watch and judge the speed of your opponent. Run alongside her on her right. Then move slightly to the left. When you feel you can reach the ball, bring the stick down firmly. You should be holding it at the end to get the maximum distance. A strong wrist will give you the strength to move the ball.

If you get the ball off your opponent's stick, you must again move quickly so she will not recover it. If you lunged one-handed, get your right hand back onto the stick. Then get over the ball as fast as you can to control it. You must either dribble or pass quickly, before your opponent tries to tackle you.

Like the straight tackle, the open-side tackle doesn't have to be

Once she has gotten her stick on the ball, she must put her right hand back on the stick. This will give her a better chance to control the ball and complete the tackle.

A successful left-hand lunge will result in a takeaway and the defensive team going back on offense.

totally successful to stop an attack. If the tackler doesn't come away with the ball, the attempted tackle could result in the ball being poked away. Or the attacker might lose her dribble or make a bad pass.

Perhaps the hardest tackle to make is the *reverse stick tackle*. It is used when a defender approaches the attacker's left side. Reverse stick tacklers must always be sure to play the ball before either their stick or body touches the opponent's stick or body. Otherwise, a foul will be called.

The tackler must move in alongside and slightly in front of the ballhandler. With the left hand at the top of the stick, she should reach across her body with the head of the stick pointing downward. She then brings it down just in front of the ball, using the left hand and wrist. If she stops the ball, the tackler can then put her right hand back on the stick and try to pull the ball away from the attacker.

52

If she can't do that, she can also try to push the ball to the other side of her opponent, then cut behind her to get control. Either way, a successful tackle will result in the defender controlling the ball. If the defender tries to poke the ball to the opposite side of the attacker, she should be sure to get her stick out of the way quickly.

Tackling is one of the best ways to stop an attack. A good defense will know how to tackle well without fouling. And an experienced player will know when to try for a tackle. It takes practice, but it's one more way to play winning field hockey.

Learning How To Be A Goalkeeper

As in other sports, a goalkeeper in field hockey must be able to move quickly. She must also be able to know ahead of time where a shot will be going. In addition, the goalkeeper must always be in top physical condition so she doesn't get tired late in the game. And she has to be able to bounce back. If she allows a score, she must not let it bother her for the rest of the game. That's part of being mentally tough.

The goalkeeper must also know the game very well. Because she can see the entire field in front of her, she is in the best position to help her teammates. So a goalie should be able to direct play, shout instructions and warnings to her teammates. In other words, she has to be a leader.

When the ball begins getting close to the striking circle, the goalie should be ready to spring into action. That means getting into the ready position. Feet are kept close together, steady and balanced, with the knees slightly bent. The hands are held out to the side, with the stick in the right hand. The stick is held about nine inches down from the top. In this position, the goalkeeper is ready to move quickly in any direction.

The first skill the goalkeeper must practice is kicking. Kick

Field hockey goalkeepers wear large leg pads, padded overshoes called kickers, a chest protector and mask. Some even wear a helmet or a helmet with a facemask attached. Padded gloves and a stick complete the uniform. But even with all this equipment, goalkeepers must be able to move quickly.

saves can be made with either foot. The more accurately the goalie can kick the ball out, the better. A goalie should practice kicking non-moving balls, moving balls, as well as balls that are bouncing. She needs a fine sense of timing.

One rule to remember. Try to kick the ball to a member of your team. If this can't be done, then kick it toward the sidelines. Never kick directly back in front of you or toward the top of the circle.

When kicking, always keep your head down and watch the ball carefully. The non-kicking foot should be placed alongside the ball. Swing your kicking leg back. Contact is made with the square toe. Follow through on the line of the ball's flight.

There are a number of good ways to practice kicking skills. One is simply to dribble the field hockey ball with both feet. Another is to kick a tennis ball against a wall. As it rebounds, kick it again. In practice, have your teammates shoot pushes, flicks and scoops at you. Soon, you'll be making kicks under game conditions.

54

A good goalie can make kick saves with either foot. The square-toed kickers make it easier to kick accurately. But the skill still takes a great deal of practice. Goalkeepers must not only kick non-moving balls, but rolling and bouncing balls as well. It is important for the goalie to always keep her eye on the ball and to follow through with every kick.

There will also be times when a goalie stops a shot with her pads, only to have the ball fall in front of her. If there is no time for a kick, she may have to *clear* the ball with her stick. This is done with a quick move, the stick held only in the right hand. The clear is made to the left with the open side of the stick. It can be a push, flick or scoop, whichever is quickest.

The most important thing in stopping different kinds of shots is not to allow a rebound. In other words, if the ball bounces off the goalie's pads back out into the striking circle, an attacker may get another quick shot. The trick is to "kill" the ball so it drops directly in front of the goalie. Then it can be cleared.

A shot coming straight at a goalkeeper may seem easy. But a goalie must still be careful. She has to make sure her body is right in front of the ball. Her knees and heels should be pressed

Clearing the ball with the stick is done with one hand. The goalie must do this quickly and can use whichever type of stroke is the quickest.

When clearing with the stick, goalkeepers should always watch the ball closely, keep their heads down and follow through. The ball should be cleared to a teammate or toward the sideline. It should never be sent back out into the striking area, where an attacker can shoot again.

together, toes slightly apart. Then she "looks" the ball right into the pads. She should bend her knees a bit more at contact. This will help the ball fall at her feet. Then she can clear it right away.

Shots along the ground that are not coming directly at the goalkeeper call for quick action. The goalkeeper must slide her foot out to the side to contact the ball. And she must do it in a way that will not allow the ball to go under her foot. In other words, the foot should not be raised off the ground during the move. It should slide along the ground as the leg is extended. The best way to stop the ball is with the padded instep of the kicker. The ball can either be kicked away or stopped and cleared.

Goalkeepers must practice this move. Sometimes they will do almost a complete split to reach the shot. They must be able to recover quickly and get right back to their feet.

A low aerial shot is probably the toughest of all to stop. The goalie must step quickly to one side or another and get her leg pads in front of the ball. Even if she takes a big step, she must

There are times when a shot will come so fast that the goalkeeper has time for only a kick save. Again, quickness and timing are important. This kind of move must be practiced often and the goalie must always stretch in warm-ups. Otherwise, a kick save like this could result in a pulled muscle.

try to keep the pad in an up and down (vertical) position if possible. She should also place her hand just to the outside of the pad to give even more coverage.

If the goalie gets the pad in front of the ball, she should try to bend her knee slightly for better control. A very good goalie can direct the ball off the pad to a nearby teammate. The ball can also be fielded with the left hand. If a hand stop is made, the ball must be dropped almost directly to the ground. It can be advanced only slightly. Then it must be cleared.

Goalies as a rule do not like to use their hands on balls coming in close to their body. That's because they would have to drop the ball directly at their feet or even under them. That would make clearing more difficult.

The hand, however, is used all the time on high shots. Once again, after the ball is caught, it must be dropped straight down. So the goalie should always try to make the catch or stop the ball a bit in front of her body. If the ball is released in front

Hand stops can be made for shots in the air. Once caught, the ball must be dropped straight down. Shots should be stopped with the hand cupped. When the ball is dropped, it can be cleared by kicking or with the stick.

of her body, she can make a kick to clear it before the ball even hits the ground. And remember, even the goalkeeper cannot raise her stick above her shoulders.

For defending against penalty shots, there is a slightly different ready position. The goalie should stand on the goal line in the middle of the goal. This time her feet should be spread just outside her shoulders. The stick should be held with both hands, the head to the right. Now she's ready to move in any direction or bring her feet together, if the shot is straight at her.

The goalkeeper may not move her feet until the ball has left the penalty stroke spot. She cannot drop her stick, raise it above her head, or use the back of the stick while saving a penalty stroke. If she does, a goal will be given to the attacking team. However, either hand may be taken off the stick to make a high or low hand save.

In general, when the ball is outside the 25-yard line, the goalie should be about eight yards from the goal. Using short, sliding steps, she should move back and forth easily, staying in line with the ball and the goal.

When the attacking team begins to advance, the goalie should drop back within about four yards of the goal. If an attacker is inside the striking circle and close to the goal line, then the goalie should be within a few yards of the post. Otherwise, a quick shot could go between the goalie and the post.

It takes work and practice to become a good goalkeeper. But it's worth it, because every team must have a top-notch goalie.

A Few Words About The Attack

As soon as any player on a team gets the ball, that team is on the attack. In general, a team should try to move the ball into the attacking end of the field very quickly. But they should do this with as few passes as possible.

If the attack starts from the defensive striking circle, the ball should quickly be passed to the side of the field away from the other players. If that first pass can't go out to the wing, then the second pass should.

Crisp passing by the halfbacks and inside forwards should help move the ball in the center of the field. Side-to-side passing also keeps the defense changing directions. And it can lead to a defensive mistake, which a good team will spot in an instant. So a good, cross-field passing game is important.

Moving the ball down the center of the field gets the job done more quickly. This gives the defense less chance to adjust because the ball can be passed in either direction. On the wing, it can only be passed toward the center of the field. The attacking team should keep itself spread out. A crowd only cuts down on the passing lanes.

Another way to move the ball is to dribble in one direction and pass in another. This also may confuse the defense. Wings should stay out near the sideline until the ball is near the striking circle. Forwards on the left side of the field must often use the reverse stick technique to receive passes. So all passes to the left must be very accurate.

Young forwards should always position themselves at about the 25-yard line. Then they are ready to start moving upfield together once the ball is cleared or changes hands. But as they get more experience, they will want to move closer to the centerline to help defend against opposing halfbacks.

In the area between the two 25-yard lines, the players have more freedom. They can create an offense with their own skills because there are no rules telling them what to do in this area. All players must be quick in receiving passes. They must know where the ball is going and get there before the defensive player. That will give them control and allow them to dribble or pass on their own.

Inside the striking circle, the forwards should always keep moving. They must make space for the player with the ball. They can fake going one way, they go the other. But they should always face the goal and look for scoring chances, even as they move back and forth and side to side. All movement within the circle should be made with the forward's left shoulder ahead of the right. That way the body is rotated slightly to the right and the player will be able to shoot faster.

There are many other things a young player must learn about attacking. Each coach will have drills and plays for the team to run. These are just the basics that every player must know to get started.

A Few Words About Defense

A defensive player must always be able to keep the ball on her stick. Instant control is the only way the defender can put her team on attack without wasting time or losing the ball again. To do this, defensive players have to be very good at fielding balls coming from any direction. They should know how to stop, receive, and control the ball.

There will be times when the defender will stop the ball. But other times she may want to just deflect it past onrushing forwards and try to pick it up again. As a rule, it is not a good idea to hit a ball without first controlling it. Uncontrolled hits can be dangerous and can draw a penalty.

Defenders should always be ready to intercept a pass. A player who is good at this knows the game very well and can anticipate where the ball will be going. The better a defensive player knows the offense, the more chance for an interception. And an intercepted pass is one of the best ways to stop a slick passing attack.

Defensive players must also keep moving. Ever time the ball is moved by the attacking team, the defense has to react. If the ball is being passed back and forth in the middle of the field, each defender must move sideways to the ball side of her opponent. That way, she is in a better position to make a tackle or intercept.

When guarding, or marking, an attacker, the defender tries to stay on the ball or goal side of her opponent. She also stays within a stick's length. This close guarding can keep another attacker from passing to the marked player. Defensive players are most likely to mark near the striking circle where the space ahead is smaller. Marking where there will be short passes gives the defense a better chance to intercept.

Marking becomes very necessary inside the circle. There, the defense is trying to stop the attacker from taking a shot on goal. By contrast, in the middle of the field, passes usually go forward. Marking only makes it easier for the offense to make those passes.

Each coach will have her own theory of defense. She will show her players the kind of defense she wants to use. That will determine how they play. Knowing the basic skills of defense and being able to stop and control a ball will give young players first things they need to play defense well.

Field hockey can be an exciting sport. It's certainly a sport that demands skill and fitness to play well. Players who learn the sport as youngsters usually continue to play. As with other sports, you'll like it better if you learn it well and become part of a team. And who knows, someday you may have the thrill of scoring the winning goal and being part of a league championship team.

Glossary

Aerial shot   A shot on goal that reaches the goalkeeper while still in the air.

Alley   The first five yards of the field in from each sideline and running parallel to the sideline.

Clear   A move by the goalkeeper to get the ball away from the goal mouth and out of scoring range. The ball can be cleared by kicking or by moving it with the stick.

Dodge   A move by a ballhandler to fake and then get past a defender.

Dribbling   The way a player moves the ball up the field by using her stick to propel it.

Flick   Stroke that lifts the ball off the ground with both power and speed.

Free hit   An unopposed hit given to the defensive team when the attacking team fouls anywhere on the field. It is also given to the attacking team when the defensive team fouls outside the striking circle.

Hit   Powerful stroke used for both passes and shots in which the stick is raised off the ground on the backswing and then driven through the ball. It is also called a drive.

Jab   A tackling technique in which the defender tries to poke the ball away from the attacker.

Jockey   Term used to describe how a defender covers her opponent without committing herself to a tackle.

Kick save   A stop of a shot on goal by the goalkeeper using her foot or leg to stop or deflect the ball.

Kilt   The type of skirt that is part of the field hockey uniform worn by many teams.

Left-hand lunge   A tackling technique in which the defender makes the tackle on the stick side of an opponent. Also called an open-side tackle.

Long hit   The way the ball is put back in play after a defender has played it over the goal line from inside the 25-yard line, but not intentionally. The hit is taken from either the sideline or the goal line, five yards from the corner flag.

Mark   A defensive maneuver in which the defender plays close enough to an opponent to prevent her from receiving a pass. It also allows her to make a tackle as soon as the opponent receives the ball. It is another term for very close guarding.

Obstruction   A foul that occurs when one player prevents an opponent from playing the ball by moving part or all of her body between the opponent and the ball.

Offsides   A violation occuring when an attacking player is nearer the opposing goal than two opponents and the ball. It is not called if the attacking player is in her own half of the field or an opponent was the last player to touch the ball.

Penalty shot   Unopposed shot on goal from seven yards away. This is given to the attacking team when a defensive player intentionally violates the rules within the striking circle. A penalty shot is also given when a defender commits a foul to stop what the umpire feels would have been an almost certain goal. Only the goalkeeper is allowed to stop a penalty shot.

Push   A very accurate and quick way of making short passes and shots by stroking the ball without a backswing.

Push back   A maneuver used to put the ball in play at the beginning of the game. The player with the ball pushes it backward to a teammate to start play. The push back takes place in the five-yard circle at the center of the field.

Push in   The way the ball is put back in play after it is hit over the sideline. The push stroke must be used.

Rebound   Any ball that bounces off the goalkeeper or the goalpost back into the field of play is a rebound.

Reverse stick   Technique in which a player turns the stick so that the head is pointing down toward the ground. This is necessary since only the flat side of the stick can be used to contact the ball.

Scoop   A stroke used to lift the ball over a group of opposing players. It's made with an upward, throwing motion. The ball should be kept in contact with the stick as long as possible.

Short corner   Name for a penalty stroke given to the attacking team after a defender has done one of three things: 1. has intentionally played the ball over her own goal line; 2. has committed a foul inside the striking circle; 3. has deliberately fouled within the 25-yard area.

Striking circle   A semi-circle with a 16-yard radius that surrounds the goal. For a goal to be scored, the attacking player must shoot the ball from within the striking circle. A shot on goal cannot come from anywhere else on the field.

Tackle   Term used to describe taking the ball away from an opponent by using the stick.

796.35
GUT
    Gutman, Bill
    Field hockey

14.95

DATE DUE			

95-9840